D0100674

Snake Safari

PATHFINDER EDITION

By Rom Whitaker

CONTENTS

Snake Safari

PHOTODISC GREEN, GETTY IMAGES

Love them or hate them, snakes are just misunderstood.

By Rom Whitaker

I am Rom Whitaker, I love snakes, and I know what you're thinking. Many people fear snakes, but when I spot one, I just want to get close and study it.

I've liked snakes since I was a kid. I met my first one—a garter snake—when I was just four years old. Ever since then, I've been smitten by snakes.

I have traveled much of the world looking for snakes. A scientist who studies snakes is called a **herpetologist**. Most of the time, I go after snakes in the wild, but sometimes, they come after me.

© SANDESH KADUR/NPL/MINDEN PICTURES

3

Reptile Royalty

My most surprising meeting with a snake took place in India. When I was camping in a forest, I saw a snake dart under a bush. Thinking it was a harmless rat snake, I leaped into the bush and grabbed it by its tail.

I couldn't have been more wrong. Hearing a strange growl, I looked up, and there was a king cobra glaring down at me. My heart was in my throat!

Hood spread, the cobra looked like it was about to strike me. That's something I didn't want to happen. The king cobra is the longest **venomous** snake. It can be 18 feet long.

When disturbed, a cobra raises its upper body and spreads special ribs to form a scary hood, which makes the snake look larger than it really is. ⟶

Usually, king cobras stay away from people, and they bite only when they are surprised. I'm sure when I grabbed its tail, I surprised this one.

I let go of the cobra's tail, but of course, I couldn't let it get away. I sprang to my feet and ran after the cobra. I captured it in my sleeping bag, so I could study it later.

Since then, king cobras have become one of my favorite snakes. I'm working to protect the forests where these amazing creatures live because I want to make sure cobras never die out, or become **extinct**.

A World of Serpents

My first encounter with a king cobra was scary, but there is little reason to be afraid of all snakes. Worldwide there are 2,400 kinds, or species, of snake, and only 270 species have a venom, or poison, that's dangerous to humans.

Most snakes get a bad rap. First of all, they are not slimy, and most of them stay away from people. In fact, snakes often help us by eating pests that can carry diseases, such as rats.

The more you know about snakes, the less scared you will be. Let's go on a snake safari and meet some of the world's most amazing snakes. We'll have to be careful because a few of them are very dangerous, and some of them could even kill you.

All snakes are reptiles, and they are related to lizards, turtles, and crocodiles. All reptiles are **cold-blooded**, which means that their bodies don't make heat. Instead, they take in heat from the air and the ground.

When a rattlesnake shakes its tail, the rattle on the end clicks and buzzes.

A snake's forked tongue collects chemical signals from the air and from objects.

Rattling Along

Many kinds of snakes call the United States home, but one stands out—the rattlesnake.

The rattlesnake is known for the rattle at the end of its tail. It uses the rattle to warn enemies that it is about to strike, but the rattle is not the only thing special about rattlesnakes.

Rattlesnakes are **pit vipers**. These snakes have a heat-sensing organ, which they can use to tell another creature's location, even in the dark.

Heat is just one way pit vipers find other creatures. Like most snakes, they can see and smell. But snakes have a special way of smelling—they use their tongues.

A snake flicks out its forked tongue to pick up scents. The forks on its tongue help the snake tell the direction the smell came from.

A Soaring Snake

Sometimes it's hard for me to tell where I might find a snake. One night I was driving in Arizona, looking for rattlesnakes. Snakes often move onto roads in the evening because the roads are warmer than the countryside. Heat from the roads helps cold-blooded snakes stay warm.

Anyway, I was driving down this road, looking for snakes, when suddenly a lyre snake fell from a tree and landed right in front of my car.

I stopped to see what had happened. The snake was lying on the road swallowing a bat. It must have caught the bat in the tree, lost its balance, and fallen. I'm not sure how the snake swallowed that whole bat, wings and all, but it did.

You might be surprised that some snakes eat bats, but snakes eat many different kinds of animals.

Snake Food

Snakes like lots of different meals. Most snakes eat birds, fish, frogs, lizards, and rats. Some larger snakes snack on monkeys.

Snakes often swallow their prey whole and alive. Venomous snakes, however, usually wait until their venom kills prey. And constrictors squeeze prey until it stops breathing; then they swallow the animal.

After a meal, most snakes rest in the sun. This helps them digest their catch, but it can also be a dangerous time. After eating, snakes are usually slow. They can't move around much, and that makes them an easy meal for another predator.

Snakes can go for days, weeks, and, in some cases, years between meals. Snakes don't need a lot of food to keep their bodies warm. That's because they are cold-blooded. Snakes also store fat in their bodies, which they can live off for a long time.

A snake uses its egg tooth to slit open its shell.

Monkey Business

It seems like everywhere I go I find snakes. During a trip to Costa Rica, I got to see lots of different snakes.

One of the snakes I caught up with was a boa constrictor. I heard some monkeys screaming. That's usually a sign that danger is near.

The monkeys were right. They had spotted a boa. Monkeys are one of its favorite foods. Anyway, I caught the snake, and it wasn't easy because boas can grow 14 feet long.

You should see a boa's mouth. It is lined with 100 sharp teeth. Its bite really hurts. This one bit me because I was too slow.

Deadly Colors

Next I met an Allen's coral snake. You really have to be careful around coral snakes because they are very venomous.

Coral snakes are also colorful. They have bands of red, black, white, or yellow along their bodies. Predators know these colors mean to stay away from the deadly snake.

If a predator does get too close, the coral snake coils around itself. This trick makes the snake's tail look like its head, and if the hungry predator goes after the tail, the snake can easily get away.

On the Road Again

I hope our snake safari has helped you look at snakes in a new way. You may never want to get as close to snakes as I do, and in fact, you shouldn't! Until you become an expert, you never know which ones are dangerous. But now that you something about snakes, I'm sure you'll want to know more.

Well, I'm off on another snake safari in India. This time I'll try not to grab a king cobra's tail—at least not accidentally.

 Why are many people afraid of snakes? Should people be afraid of snakes?

Colorful bands →
scare away
predators.

Sniffing for Snakes

The Louisiana pine snake is in lots of trouble. It may be one of the rarest snakes around. It lives only in pine forests in Louisiana and Texas.

Foresters want to protect the pine snake, but they don't even know how many of the snakes there are.

You see, the pine snake spends most of its time underground, and the foresters can't count the snakes because they can't find them.

Foresters are turning to another animal to help count the snakes. They want to train dogs to sniff them out. Dogs have a great sense of smell, and they might even be able to smell a snake in its underground den. That could help foresters learn how many pine snakes are around.

Wordwise

cold-blooded: animal that does not make its own body heat

extinct: completely gone

herpetologist: scientist who studies snakes

pit viper: snake with organs that sense heat

venomous: poisonous

Snakes

Alive!

There are many kinds of snakes. They live in many different places—on land, in water, under the ground, and in trees high above. But all snakes have one thing in common—they have all adapted to their environment. Their bodies and their behaviors help them stay alive.

Blending In

The world is a dangerous place for snakes. They have many predators, or animals that like to eat them, so snakes often need to play it safe.

One way snakes stay safe is the color of their skin. How can color help snakes? It lets them blend in with their environment.

For example, some snakes live in green places. They are surrounded by green leaves and vines. A snake that is red or yellow would stand out among all that green, but a green snake fits right in.

Other snakes live where things are mostly brown. What kind of snake could hide among sticks and dirt? You guessed it! A snake that is brown and looks like a twig.

Coloring is a good disguise, because it helps some snakes hide from a predator's eyes.

Seeing Green.
The color of these vine snakes makes them hard to spot against green leaves.

Handy Hideaways

Camouflage may keep some snakes out of harm's way, but it's not the only way they stay off the menu. Snakes also rely on their shape to keep them safe.

Snakes don't have legs, so they can't outrun a predator. They don't have arms to beat animals back, but their sleek bodies do give them an advantage.

Snakes can hide in their tightest of spots. They can slither between rocks, they can wedge themselves into crevices and cracks, and they can hide in holes and hollow trees. Bigger animals can't squeeze into these handy hideaways, so snakes stay safely inside. After a while, predators get bored and wander off in search of an easier meal.

Hiding Out. Snakes have skinny bodies that let them squeeze into small hiding spots. When a predator leaves, the snake can slither safely away.

Facing Danger

Some snakes face danger head-on. This is true of some big snakes. Instead of hiding, they coil into a ball. Their meaty bodies protect their heads.

Other snakes try to bluff their way to safety. That's the case with the hognosed snake. It uses every trick in the book.

First, it flattens its neck because it wants to look like a dangerous cobra. If that doesn't work, the snake pretends to get sick. Sometimes it even throws up or begins to bleed.

Finally, the hognosed snake stages its own death. It curls and twitches, and then it lies perfectly still and pretends to be dead.

Believe it or not, this acting job actually works. Many predators won't make a snack out of this "sick" snake.

Fighting Back

When all else fails, some snakes go on the attack. They fight back with one of the only weapons they have: their fierce fangs.

Predators know that a snake bite is nothing to sneeze at. It can really hurt. Some snakes have venom, or poison, in their bite, and that venom can kill a predator.

A few venomous snakes don't even have to bite. They just spit. Their venom can shoot as far as eight feet away! Spitting snakes aim for the eyes. They try to blind a predator, and then they can slither away to safety.

Snakes have many different defenses to keep themselves safe. Camouflage colors are only just the start. The name of the game is staying alive.

All in a Ball. This green snake protects itself by curling into a tight ball. That keeps its head safe from a predator's bite.

Coral snakes are poisonous. They can kill large animals with one bite. Their bright colors warn animals to stay away.

King snakes are not poisonous, and yet they are brightly colored, too. In fact, they look a lot like dangerous coral snakes.

Most predators don't know the difference, so they stay away from king snakes, too.

Animals like the king snake are called mimics. Mimics are copycats because they look like another kind of animal. Their looks help them survive.

Fangs for Fighting. Some snakes use their fangs to fight off predators. The fangs of this rattlesnake are sharp and filled with venom.

Snakes

It's time to sink your fangs into some questions about snakes.

1 What is a scientist who studies snakes called?

2 What does it mean to be cold-blooded?

3 Why can snakes go so long between meals?

4 How do snakes protect themselves?

5 Why do some people want to keep snakes from becoming extinct?

© PHOTODISC